The Anxious Entrepreneur

"You have got to win in your mind before you win in your life"

- *John Addison*

The Anxious Entrepreneur

A quick guide to starting a business that you are passionate about in spite of fear, funds or inexperience.

Jason Staniforth

No part of this publication can be reproduced or distributed in any form, whether photocopied, recorded, or any other electronic means, unless prior written permission is given by the publisher and/ or author.

Brief quotations may be allowed in the instance of reviews and for other non-commercial purposes.

If you would like permission to utilise any part of this publication, please use the contact details at the back of this book.

This book is written based on the experiences of the author and, although we have taken every precaution to ensure the accuracy of the information here within, neither the author nor the publisher assume any responsibility for errors or omissions. Again, neither assume any responsibility, nor liability, for damages resulting from the use of the information contained within this book.

[Edited February 2019]

DEDICATION

I'd like to dedicate this book to my Mom, Amanda, the kindest and most caring woman I know who, for a large portion of my childhood, went without, so that I wouldn't have to.

To my stepdad, Paul, who continued to drive life lessons into me from an early age, even though I didn't appreciate them at the time; those lessons have helped me ever since.

And to my partner, Naomi, who has supported me through one of the toughest times of my life and has been a constant reminder of why I should face my demons head on and refuse to settle for 'average'.

I'd also like to thank everyone who told me that I would never make anything of myself, to past friends that mistook my kindness for weakness, and to the people in the world who publicly thrive on the differences and weaknesses of others; you may have built walls around me for a while, but it's because of people like you, that people like me can now break through walls.

FOREWARD

This book is a fantastic step-by-step guide on how to overcome the obstacles that life can throw at you whilst giving you the tools to create something great from the things that you care about most.

Jay's book stood out to me as, usually, when you read a book about self-help, the author has already made their millions and is telling their story from a point of comfort and serenity; the beautifully rare position of this book, and Jay's story, is that he is still on his journey, and he is still stumbling and learning, like many of you.

If you are at the start of your journey, or if you are being held back from the path that you want to take, this book will help you to understand that regardless of any challenges that life can throw at you, there is always a way to get through it.

Knowing Jason as a colleague, as a teacher, as a student, and as a friend, I've seen how he has gone from, in his own way, sabotaging his own success, to using the steps outlined in this book to climb out of the traps that he found himself in, to being one step closer to the life that he dreams of.

This is a great example of how to be honest with yourself about what's really going on in your life so that you can address it head-on to take your life, and your business, to the next level.

As an entrepreneur, I can honestly thank Jason for being there at the start of my journey as his motivation, his knowledge, and his drive played a pivotal part in my early success. I have built several multi-million-pound companies and created a property portfolio of over £4 million, in just 18 months, using zero of my own money. I am now an international trainer and coach, following my mission to assist over 20 million people to be free financially, emotionally, spiritually, and mentally, by the year 2037.

I am so pleased that Jason has found a way to offer support and encouragement and translate it into a step-by-step guide in this book that will help you to do the same for yourself, and eventually for others.

Mark Harvey

Property Investor, Sales Trainer, International Speaker & Coach

For more information on Mark Harvey and the Real Life brand, you can visit his website:

www.reallifesalestraining.com

INTRODUCTION

I want this book to be short, sweet, and straight to the point. Many of the techniques in this book have been created from what I have learnt at seminars that I have attended, courses that I have taken, entrepreneurs that I have engaged with, and books that I have read; I've then coupled these lessons with my own experiences to create a strategy that can be replicated by any budding entrepreneur to find the success that you deserve – regardless of the anxiety and self-doubt that is currently holding you back.

Before you start this book, I want you to understand that I am not a world-renowned entrepreneur (I'd have charged a lot more for this book if I was ha-ha), I am not a multi-millionaire, and I am not a guru of any sort... yet – give it some time.

However, what I am is a driven and determined individual with entrepreneurial traits, a burning passion for personal growth, marketing, and helping others to succeed, both professionally and personally. I overcame years of severe social anxiety to allow myself to step out from the shadows and to make something of myself; to become someone that I could be proud of.

I've now helped a long list of people to start their own businesses and to become more successful in what they do. I've helped people in markets such as luxury vehicles and automotive repairs, cosmetics & beauty, fitness, logistics, consultancy & coaching, charity, marketing, event management, entertainment, and property investment – I've even worked with an Olympic Diver and a celebrity personal trainer!

I've quickly come to realise that, yes, it does help to work with someone that knows the industry you are hoping to work in, or already work in, but there are certain principles, a framework if you will, that you must follow in order to start or grow a business and to get things moving in the right direction – this book looks at those steps.

Don't see this book as a "do it this way or you will fail" type of book, but rather take the lessons that you believe will work for you, chop and change them as you see fit, and refer back to them for inspiration or guidance as you progress on your journey.

It would be great for you to share your thoughts and update me on your journey as you progress, so, if you're reading this right now, I have a quick task for you...

TASK

Jump onto Twitter or Instagram and send me a photo or a video of you holding this book.

You can tweet it to me at @jaystaniforth or get me on Instagram with Jaystaniforth and use the hashtag #AnxiousEntrepreneur

CONTENTS

Part One - What is stopping you from starting?
The story behind how I started out and the reason you can make a living doing what you love

Part Two - Getting started and planning your success
How to commit to your goals and guarantee that you follow through with your actions

Part Three - Finding your passion
The process you need to follow in order to identify exactly which of your passions you can turn into a profitable business

Part Four - How to stand out in a crowd
Mastering your elevator pitch and talking about your business offering with passion

Part Five - Making your business, social
The steps that you should take to effectively promote yourself and your business with social media

Part Six - Blog like a pro – for beginners
How to structure your blogs to create interest and demand engagement

Part Seven - Email mastery
Tips, techniques and templates for creating emails that demand attention and engagement from your mailing lists

Part Eight - Success Logging
The most effective way to self-manage your own goals and personal learning

Part Nine - Top tips summary
Top 10 tips to mastering your business

Part Ten - Useful tools
Links and extra social bits that I find helpful and you might find helpful, too

Summary
A few final words from Jay Staniforth

Part One

WHAT IS STOPPING YOU FROM STARTING?

INTRODUCTION

When I was at school, I never really knew what I wanted to do as a job; when I asked my friends what they wanted to do, they gave me a mixture of the classic answers that you'd expect when asking kids what they want to be when they grow up: footballers, rock stars, famous actors, or the same answer that you get when you ask teenagers, and even adults, today, "I want to be rich".

These career choices, or dreams, didn't really excite me; not because I didn't think I would enjoy them, but more that I didn't think they were achievable for a normal kid like me. Maybe you can relate to this?

In my mind, I was just average Jay – and that was me, I was average. I was average at most of the things I did, I wasn't ashamed or embarrassed that I was average at everything, in fact, it was quite the opposite.

I was fully aware that there was always someone better than me at whatever the task or activity was, but I suffered heavily from social anxiety, and being average provided me with the sanctity of what I called the 'human haze'. Basically, I didn't particularly stand out for any good reason or for any bad reason, I just blended in, and that kept the attention off me.

As a child, this is an incredibly negative and damaging approach to have to life and, not surprisingly, it was this belief that held me back for much of my school life; the belief that no matter what I did there would always be someone better than me, someone who would stand out more. I rationalised this by accepting that it was ok as it made sense to avoid any form of success or attention because of my fear of social situations. Can you imagine living your life at 50% effort through fear of getting attention?

As I moved into my early teens, I had become part of a small friend group. Surprisingly, some of my friends were popular kids in school, which completely confused me as I couldn't understand why they wanted me to be part of their group.

In time, it quickly became evident that, although I was part of the group, I was the butt of most of the jokes, the cruel names and childish songs that were sang; "Cadet Sergeant Doofy" was one that I remember – they called me this because I had joined the Air Training Corps.

Being called these names and being criticised for the way that I looked made me feel like I was a kind of 'cool-person marker', with me being a lesser person, I made them appear to be that much more popular, or cooler, in comparison.

My best friend at the time, he was also part of the small group of friends, was actually one of the people who ridiculed me the most – I found this to be the most hurtful as it was often when we were in the group that I became a target for him yet, when we were alone together, we got on great and I almost felt like an equal. I knew deep down that he didn't mean anything by it and that he was just playing up to the crowd, but it still crushed me every time he called me a name or made up a song, because although he would only mock me once or twice, it was the rest of the group that would continue the verbal torture.

I developed a type of defensive humour whereby I'd mock myself during group situations – I did this so that I was, in effect, getting to the punch-line first, which massively reduced the amount of negative attention I received. I knew this wasn't a solution for my problems, but it was a temporary fix that I hoped would get me through the next few years at school.

So where did it all change for me?

If I think back to a specific situation, the situation that changed everything, it would be this;

One day on the school field, I found myself surrounded by a group of boys that had decided they didn't like me, for no known reason - I just assumed I was different and that was enough to justify it to them.

The friend stood next to me had obviously seen what was about to happen, as the group approached, and he conveniently kicked his football away so that he could remove himself from the situation.

I stood there, alone, surrounded by 9 or 10 boys who were hurling abuse at me, threatening me with comments about 'knocking me out' and 'breaking my nose', 'smashing me in' and other equally 'friendly' statements.

I remember it as clear as day; in that moment, everything seemed to move slowly, their voices muffled and my focus on nothing but myself and my own thoughts. It was as if time had slowed down, almost stopping, but only I was aware.

I could feel the blood rushing around my body, my heart rate increasing as it pumped my blood through my veins, powering the rush of adrenaline that was building up inside of me. My fingers began to vibrate, hands shaking inside of my pockets, trembling with confusion, shock, and fear; unimaginable thoughts were vigorously switching through my mind like a movie on fast-forward... until it suddenly stopped.

A sense of calm poured through my body, like the feeling you get when you finally stop after a period of intense exercise, it was as if their words didn't matter, they meant absolutely nothing to me – I had no fear, no insecurity, and no self-doubt.

In that moment, something occurred to me. I realised that no matter what I did, no matter how much I tried to hide, someone, somewhere, would find me, and whether it was for a good reason, or a bad reason, I had no control of it - I could only control how I reacted to it.

After what seemed like a long time, my focus returned to the situation I was in which, luckily for me, dissipated quite quickly as the boys verbally assaulting me were mostly full of empty threats and they eventually left me alone.

But this was an eye-opener for me. I had stood there, alone, with 9 or 10 people hurling abuse at me, and 20 or 30 onlookers with their attention lasered onto me like a series of snipers on a target, I was even abandoned by my friend in the moment that I needed him the most - and I was fine.

In that moment, I decided that the next time I had the attention of that many people, or even more, I want it to be for a reason that I have chosen to be noticed – on my own terms!

It was a bold thought to have, but I was determined to remove this insecurity, this lack of self-belief, and this constant anxiety from my life.

As time went on, things did improve for me. Although I was still quite reserved and reluctant to let myself fully shine, I did begin to excel in several areas; football, running, drawing, and I even showed signs of leadership in my role at the Air Training Corps.

For a period of time I really enjoyed running. Competitive running symbolised a turning point that I had made in my life, instead of running away from my thoughts, my fears, and even physically running from those that fed off my weakness, I made the choice to run, but instead of running away, I'd be running towards my goals, towards success, and towards a bigger, better and more confident version of me.

In my younger years, this came out in the activities available to me at school, but as I started to get older, I began to find passions in my life, some small and some short-lived, but nonetheless, they were things that I was passionate about.

I turned my focus to earning positive attention, attention that I was given because people around me deemed my actions to be impressive, and this is where I gained my first life lesson around the importance of a niche.

At this point I had started skateboarding and I was, you guessed it, average. But average was not acceptable to me anymore – I wanted to be noticed for it.

Knowing that I didn't have much chance of standing out for performing the simple skateboarding tricks, I decided that I would focus on something that no one else in my area was doing – my niche, if you will.

Now, I haven't covered this bit yet, but years before the school field incident, I still suffered with anxiety, and I didn't feel comfortable with the competitive sports that the boys played, so I would hang around with the girls and do handstands against walls – this is when I discovered that I was pretty good at walking on my hands and balancing – so here comes the 'tilt'...

I decided to make it my mission to learn how to skate along on my skateboard and then, whilst the skateboard was moving with me on top of it, push myself up into a handstand and remain there until the skateboard lost momentum.

And I did it! Not just once, either. I could do it easily, and for long periods of time. My friends were in awe of my talent. I was the only person that I knew who could perform this trick, other than the famous skaters that we all aspired to be.

This was another break-through for me. I had discovered that I didn't have to be the best at everything to get noticed, I just had to be the best at something, and the tighter the niche, the easier it was to do.

This break-through led me on to other passions, and these passions helped me to step out of my comfort zone, they helped me to push for things that I once thought were out of my reach and above my ability. My love for these activities meant that it was harder for me to accept missing out than it was for me to face my fear of the attention that I might get as a result of them – it was only when I discovered my passions that I was actually able to start living.

TASK

Finding Your Passion

I want you to think about your dream job.

For many of you, that won't be the job that you have right now, and that's fine, but think about why you aren't doing what you would love to be doing.

Now think about the job that you currently have. If it isn't your dream job, do you really enjoy it? You may answer yes, but I want you to think about this, look deep into your heart, do you 'really' enjoy it, or is there something else that you would rather be doing, something you are passionate about perhaps?

So, a good place to start is to ask yourself this question.

If you could do any job, as a career, and there was no chance that you would fail, what would you do?

When you are passionate about what you do for a living it doesn't seem like work. Every hour that you work feels like fun.

Sounds like a dream doesn't it?

This is what I want for you and it's all possible. Using what I have learnt about marketing, sales, goal setting, psychology and mind-set, I want to help you to turn your passion into a business, a career, and a lifestyle.

Using my own experiences, failures and successes, as well as those of others I have worked and shared experiences with, I will help you to discover how your passion can become your career.

All I ask from you, is that you take action.

If you have any doubts about your ability to make such a dramatic change in your life, just remember this,

"Whether you think you can, or you think you can't, you're right".

...and the hardest part is simply starting.

BONUS TASK

I know that it's hard to just change and start moving in a different direction to what you have been going in for so long, and I can appreciate that reducing or removing your anxiety and self-doubt is not as easy as saying,

"Yep, that's me done with being anxious... world... COME AT ME!"

So, I wanted to share a bonus exercise that you can do to begin to build your self-confidence and to strengthen your mind as to what you should be focusing on.

Note: To this day, I still do this exercise every single day. I have created a programme called Success Logging – I talk about this later in the book – whereby I have a comfort zone or gratitude challenge to complete every day, followed by a self-confidence and self-promotion activity in the form of a LIVE video on social media.

You can find out more about Success Logging here:

https://empire-consulting-group.com/free-access

The bonus task is this;

Write down 30 actions or activities that make you feel uncomfortable, anxious, or self-conscious. Cut them out individually, fold them up, and place them into a jar or a bowl.

Every morning, you are going to pick one of the pieces of paper out of the jar/bowl and read the challenge.

You have the entire day to complete that challenge.

At the end of the day, you are going to go LIVE on Facebook, YouTube, Instagram, or whatever social vehicle you choose, and share your experience of the challenge that you undertook for that day.

You must do this every single day for at least 30 days.

Repeatedly taking action with something that causes you to face your anxieties will, over time, remove those anxieties and replace them with increased confidence.

After the 30 days, you should create another 30 actions, and repeat the process.

I recommend that you never stop this and that you make it a part of who you are and your daily routine.

NOTE:

If you're struggling to think of what challenges you should create for yourself, you can join the Private Facebook Group for The Anxious Entrepreneur and ask us directly for some guidance.

https://www.facebook.com/groups/theanxiousentrepreneur/

Below: An example of the Success Log Day Page that I follow. I have put a box around the challenge and live section.

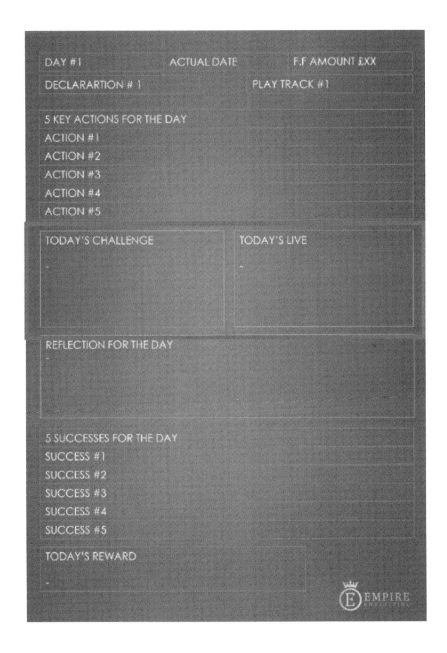

Part Two

GETTING STARTED AND PLANNING YOUR SUCCESS

I wanted to share a lesson with you that I learnt from a conference I attended in London, early 2017. I was told that planning, rewarding yourself both physically and mentally, and the reason that breaking down your big goals into smaller more achievable goals, was that it will guarantee you a level of success. You may wish to return to this section after reading part three, but understanding the lesson here is incredibly important.

Maybe you can relate to this, or maybe you can't, but people tend to be bad at creating what could be described as the perfect life, or the life that they see as being ideal.

This is because most people, like me before, don't have any plans in place, they have no goals, no set direction, and no way of measuring anything – so, as a result, they leave it to chance and, inevitably, most people never achieve it.

If this sounds like your life, then I'm sorry to say but you are in serious trouble.

I'm joking. Don't panic, you're not alone. This book is designed for people just like you and to help you find comfort in knowing that you've already taken one of the most important steps you can take by buying this book – you've acknowledged the issue and taken action.

Kudos my friend!

When people do make a plan, or set a goal, it's often the case that they focus on money and, as a result, providing they stick to that plan, they earn lots of money, but their health, their body, and their family time will be sacrificed as they spend so much time working. Once again, this was me, working 8am until 8pm and getting no further in life. Committing this much time to someone else's business, someone else's dream, and leaving no time for your own ventures, your own learning and your own development, will only lead to a lack of fulfilment.

On the flip side, you have the people who have a good work-life balance, good health, they're in great shape and get lots of family time, but they sacrifice their financial dreams in order to achieve a "happy" balance, as I like to call it.

At the seminar, I learnt and have since lived by the rule that there are 7 steps to improving your life and achieving your goals.

The purpose of these steps is to work out what you *really* want in life.

So, let's start;

What is it that you really want, not what would be nice to have, or what would be a bit of fun but what would make your life complete? What would make you incredibly happy and completely fulfilled?

If you're anything like me, and like most of the people I speak to, you'll have no idea as to what you truly want out of life; so, it's important that you spend some time working it out. This should be the absolute first step that you take, especially if you want to avoid taking 1 step in 10 directions, or 10 steps in the wrong direction – that's a lot of time wasted and I'm here to help you to avoid that and to accelerate your success.

Clarity is a key factor for achieving success, you must know what it is that you want and the reasons *why* you want what you say you want.

The key word to focus on here is *you*.

What is it that *you* want? – not what your family want you to do, not what your friends want you to do, not even what your life partner wants you to do – you must focus on what *you* want to do.

This is an area that I made mistakes in, I wasted a lot of time trying to please my parents, and even more time trying to become what I thought was socially acceptable to be – it was this that led me down the path to failure – multiple times.

When you aren't passionate about the thing you're dedicating your attention to, or your *focus*, and you haven't established a genuine *why* for doing it, it's all too easy to give up as soon as things get tough.

It's a good idea to spend some time thinking about this. Ignore what you wanted in the past, what you wanted as a child or as a teenager and focus on what you want *now*.

Maybe you'd like to have your own business, maybe you want to travel, perhaps you want to start a family or change profession; whatever it is, you need to be specific, always be specific.

Being specific will help to present you with both clarity and direction; having both of these in place will allow you to assign realistic and achievable goals to set you on your way.

There are 8 key areas that you can apply these steps to:

1. Finance & Money
2. Business & Career
3. Relationships & Love
4. Health & Wellness
5. Recreation & Rest
6. Education & Personal Development
7. Personal Environment & Surroundings
8. Charity & Contribution

I've always found that writing stuff down helps me to *focus* and stay on track; in the past I would just use a notepad and create lists, but now, I use something called a Success Log. As I mentioned in the last chapter, I cover the Success Log later in this book, but the idea is that I utilise a book for an entire year to create lists, write down goals, statements and sayings that I live by, and tick off successes and achievements as they occur. I'm going to take a stab in the dark here and assume that you don't have your own Success Log, so I've created space within this book for you to write your answers down.

If you're the type of person that would prefer not to write in your book, or you are reading an eBook version of this book, feel free to use a notepad.

When completing this section, focus on just one step at a time, pick whichever is the most important to you right now, and then write down 1 specific area that you want to focus on.

TASK

The Steps

Step 1

Selecting your area of focus.

Select your key area to focus on, e.g. Business & Career. Then write down specifically what it is that you want to do, for example, *I want to set up my own marketing consultancy that helps entrepreneurs who suffer with self-doubt and anxiety to take their business to 6 or 7 figures, whilst providing me with a passive income of £10,000 per month.*

....
....
....
....
....
....
....
....
....
....

Step 2

Why do you want to do this?

You must know your reason for wanting to do this, there must be a *why*. Without this, it will be all too easy to give up when the going gets tough.

For example, *I want to earn enough money from a business that I am passionate about so that I have the freedom to travel and experience the world with my family whilst we are all here.*

Once you have discovered your reason why, you need to ask yourself 3 questions:

1. Why do you think this important to you?
2. What is the pain that you will feel if you fail?
3. What will you feel like once you succeed?

Example answers for this are:

1. *I want enough money to be free, but it must be money earnt doing something that I enjoy.*
2. *My freedom will be restricted by finances and my employer, working towards someone else's dream who would also control my income.*
3. *I will feel empowered, in control of my life and free. This would increase my levels of motivation to do more and to help others.*

Write your answers down below.

1
....
....
....
....
....

2
....
....
....
....
....

3
....
....
....
....
....

Step 3

What do you think the reason is that you don't already have what you want?

Understanding this is tough, and most people don't ever consider this, but it is often the missing link to success.

If you're missing this success link with this goal, then it's likely that you are missing the same success link in other areas of your life.

For example, *I have prevented myself from taking action due to fear of failure and loss of money, whilst spreading myself too thin on too many projects at one time.*

....
....
....
....
....
....
....

Step 4

Your strategy for success.

This is the section where you define what your plan is going to be along with the steps you are going to take.

When I first completed this step, I tried to merge my existing plan with my new plan in the hope that I could change very little but get a better result – let me save you a shed load of time in saying that if you think using an old or existing plan is the right thing to do, then think again!

You need a new plan and a new approach. If your old or existing plan was going to work then you would have already succeeded, so think *new*.

Your old strategy will not deliver new results. So, let's work on a new strategy.

How are you going to do this and what's your new approach going to be?

For example, *I am going to focus on better understanding Facebook advertising by learning from a recent book, blog or video. I will directly approach new businesses with this knowledge to try and generate revenue.*

....
....
....
....
....
....
....
....
....
....

Step 5

What is your first action going to be?

Goal setting is something that I do religiously now, but, back in the day when I first started out, I would think of what I wanted to do, then I'd think about how I could do it, then I'd think about it some more, and some more, and then some more – and more often than not, I'd take no action at all and the 'goal' that I had thought of fails before it even hits the notepad.

More business ideas fail before they even start, and it's because of fear, anxiety or self-doubt that this happens!

Stop thinking about it and just fricking do something about it! I'll say that again to make sure it's sank in…

Stop thinking about it and just fricking do something about it!

The first action you take will provide you with momentum and taking action will mean that momentum is working in your favour, it's working with you. Once you have momentum, magic starts to happen!

Let me give you an example; *I am going to research and source a book on Facebook advertising that I can learn Facebook advertising techniques from.*

The best bit of advice I can give you here is to pick something simple, something easy.

If you make your first goal too difficult, and you fail, then you've failed before you've even started. By making small, easy to reach goals and increasing the difficulty as the overall goal begins to materialise, you're setting yourself up for success.

Remember, keep the first few steps simple and easy, because if it is easy, then you are going to do it.

....
....
....
....
....
....

Step 6

Committing yourself to the goal.

In this step, you are holding yourself accountable to the goal that you have created for yourself. This is to ensure that you stick to it.

Think about the action you need to take and then write it down in your notepad or in the section below. Once you have written it down, it is set and cannot be changed or altered.

We're not quite at the stage of trusting each other yet, are we, so I want to add in another layer of accountability. I want you to pick a person from your phonebook that you are friends or associates with but tend not to socialise with.

Once you have picked this person, you need to contact them by telephone and tell them what you are doing and why you are doing it.

Explain that you want to make them your accountability partner and that, should they accept this responsibility, you will check back in with them on X date to give a progress update.

Write this information below, including who your accountability partner is going to be.

....
....
....
....
....
....

Once you get the hang of this, you can consider using the Success Log as this teaches self-accountability and is one of the best ways to guarantee you take continuous action. Again, more on the Success Log later.

Step 7

Rewarding yourself for your successes.

During my studies into Human Psychology, I learnt a lot about reward-based behaviour, but you may also recognise some of what I'm about to mention from your childhood.

As a child, most of us will recall our parents praising us for good behaviour with treats such as sweets and toys; this is because, as humans, we are designed with an innate need for gratification – and we often want it quickly.

The reason that our parents reward us for good behaviour is that it acts as a positive reinforcer to encourage us to continue this favourable behaviour. Another example of this is giving you points in arcade games or level numbers.

As you perform a task well, or you complete a percentage of the game, you are instantly rewarded with points or progression to the next level. This encourages you to play for longer and repeat the behaviour. It works the same in business and in life; you need to reward the behaviour that you want to repeat.

Here is an example of what I do once I have achieved something. I purchase a pick 'n' mix tub of my favourite sweets and eat them whilst watching a movie with my partner (I use this one a lot as I love sweets).

Write down your reward

....
....
....
....
....
....

What's next?

So, now that you have your first action planned out and you have a good understanding as to why you want to do this, you need to make sure that you complete all actions in the time that you set yourself. Missing the deadline is another version of failure.

Remember, if you let it slip once, you will let it slip again… and if you do this, those 'slips' will begin to appear in other areas of your life and failure will become a part of who you are.

How you do anything is how you do everything, so pick your accountability partner, stick to your deadlines, and utilise this process for as many areas of your life as you can.

Some people I have done this exercise with have been removing themselves from a 'bad crowd' and so felt they were unable to find an accountability partner, in which case, I'd suggest getting yourself a coach.

Coaches can be a great tool as they can help to identify your 'why nots' and help with your strategy whilst keeping you accountable to complete what you say you will complete.

Working in this way will help you to track your progress and plan out future actions; in the same way that people measure and track gym progress, marketing activities, or lap times; what you track and measure, you can improve.

***

If you are struggling to select an accountability partner or a coach, you can connect with me on social media or email me to take advantage of my coaching and support services – these details can be found at the end of this book.

Part Three

FINDING YOUR PASSION AND YOUR *WHY*

The *'Why'* that pushed me to buy my first house

I remember back to my early twenties when I was living at my parents' house; my step dad ran his house like a military camp.

Everything had a place and god forbid should it not be returned there after use. The entire house was spotless, language was kept in order and I wasn't even allowed to wear hoodies with band names on.

At the time it felt like prison, like most teenagers or young adults still living at home, I had the 'stop ruining my fun' mentality and the obvious reaction to this was to rebel as much as I could – out of me and my older brother, yes, I was the naughty one.

I look back now and wish I'd taken more notice of the advice I was given. I'm still thankful for the lessons that did stick with me, but also for the pressure that it put me under.

At the time, I was incredibly unhappy at home and, as a result, after I had finished my University degree in Psychology, I spent the next 12 months working out how I could get out of the house as quickly as possible.

This desire to escape my parents' house was a direct result of me pushing so hard to set up my own business to be able to earn enough money to move out. I started building simple websites for small businesses and, within the year, I had saved enough money to buy my first house. It was empowering to see just how easily I could make money – but it didn't last.

Once I'd moved into my first house, I'd stopped looking for businesses to build more websites for and over time I stopped working on it completely. I told myself that I was just focusing on my day job, but now I realise that this was just a bull crap story I was telling myself to justify my lack of action.

The reason I had actually stopped working on my business, and this only makes sense to me now, is that I had lost my reason *why*. When I was living at home, I was determined to be there for as short a time as possible. I would think about the arguments my stepdad and I would have on an almost daily basis;

"Have some respect, stop treating this place like a hotel..." he would shout at me.

"Well stop charging me like it's one, then!" I'd yell back at him, referring to the £100 a month board I was made to pay – that's the kind of smart-arse remarks he had to deal with, the poor man!

As soon as I was out of my parent's house, my drive to make money had disappeared. Although I enjoyed making the websites and meeting new clients, I wasn't passionate about them, it wasn't what I could see myself doing for the rest of my life – in addition to this, it was hard work and incredibly time-consuming. Without my reason *why*, it was too easy to give up when it began to get tough and sacrifices were having to be made – this is what I want to help you to avoid, because when things get tough, anxiety and self-doubt sets in.

After a lot of research and a whole line of dropped businesses, I discovered a way to maximise your chance of success when creating a business from your passions, and it can be done in 6 simple steps.

TASK

Six simple steps to finding the passion that has business potential

For this task you are going to need a notepad and a pen – that is all!

NOTE: This exercise is mostly for those that are not currently running their own business, however, it could still be a good exercise to complete as it may uncover some interesting results for you.

Step 1
Create a list of everything that you have a passion for – so this could be anything from make-up or football, to social media or teaching.

The important thing here is that it is a true passion of yours and not just something that you enjoy from time to time; take your time with this, spend some serious time thinking about what it is that you're truly passionate about.

Step 2
From this list, cross out the items that you aren't skilled at and aren't knowledgeable about – for example, if you love football, but are not very good at playing it and you

have very little knowledge on it, you would remove it from your list.

Step 3
Your list should be shrinking down nicely by this point but we're about to cross a few more items off.
Now that you have a list of passions that you are skilled at and/or knowledgeable about, think carefully about which ones you can monetise. Those that you don't think will fit into this category, cross out.

Step 4
Now think about the items that you have left in your list, is there a demand for them?

If not, is there a particular niche that you could focus on? I gave the example of my handstand skateboarding trick to make me stand out.

Another example, there's no shortage of cooking vlogs but your niche is creating a vlog on how to bake birthday cakes into the shape of everyday objects.

Spend some time thinking about what you could do in each of the areas that you have left in your list and where you might be able to find demand. If some of the items leave you at a blank, cross them off.

Step 5

Now that you are down to your final few items, it's time to think about which one appeals to you the most.

You need to write down the potential that each item has in terms of the business that you can create with it, the product or service that you can offer, the way in which you can deliver it, and the money that you can charge.
Once you have these written down, spend some serious time considering which item is the best option for you. You may even wish to consider combining a couple of the items together, for instance, if you are passionate about teaching and passionate about writing, an option would be to create a unique way or a specific niche that you can teach people to write for.

Step 6

Your *why*. The fact that you are about to embark on a business venture with something that you are truly passionate about is a great step for any budding entrepreneur to take, but this might not be enough to ensure your success.

Although there is never any guarantee of success in business, having a *why* certainly makes it difficult to fail – because you only fail when you stop trying, and with a strong enough *why*, it's harder to face the pain of giving up, than it is to face the difficulties of carrying on.

This task is simple to follow but can be quite difficult to complete. Make sure you take your time with it, think about your answers. This could be the start of your new life as a more confident and determined entrepreneur and as a business owner who acts in spite of fear, funds, or inexperience.

The rest of this book is going to guide you through some key points to help you become more confident in the actions that you must take to promote yourself and, ultimately, succeed in your business – but remember this;

No amount of reading is going to make you succeed, it will certainly help you, it will expand your knowledge, teach you new things and guide you, but only you can make this work.

You need to be the driving force behind your business, and this is why taking your time over the first few sections of this book is so important.

So, only if you are committed to making this work, and only if you can look at everything you have written down so far and can hand-on-heart say,

"Yes, this is my dream, my passion, my purpose and now my goal, and I am fully committed to making this work, no matter what challenge I face, no matter how many times I stumble or fall, this is my destiny, this is the first step to

creating a new me, a better me, and a more successful version of me",

then let's begin. (I have included the above affirmation at the back of this book for quick access in the future).

Part Four

HOW TO STAND OUT IN A CROWD

Naming Your Company

Naming your company is often given more weight than it deserves; I have set up many businesses in the past where I focused on the name for literally months, some of those businesses remained as ideas because of this, and although the name is important and does have some impact on how memorable your company is, in the first instance, especially if you are struggling for a name, just use a name that states your industry.

For example, Leicester Gardening Services – if you were a landscape gardener, or, Fast Food Marketing – if you were a marketing agency specifically focused at helping the restaurant sector.

Another great way to create a name for your business is to simply say what your product is; one of my favourite examples is that of Dollar Shave Club.

These guys, in my opinion, create some of the most genius marketing campaigns on the web, although we can save that for another discussion, but in terms of their name, you know exactly what they do – discount shaving equipment starting at one dollar.

So, they are some of the things to consider when naming your business, but what should you avoid when naming your business?

The first thing to avoid doing is using a name that is difficult to spell. When you have a name that is hard to spell, people searching for your website or information around your business might struggle to locate it; they may even stumble across a competitor's page whilst searching for you, and you definitely do not want that.

I would also avoid using words that could potentially have another meaning in another language, particularly if you are planning on selling internationally.

An example is the Poland-made "Fart Bar" (I still laugh every time I think of this). In Poland, where this candy bar is made, the name translates to "lucky bar." As you can imagine, this bar wouldn't sell so well in the UK or US markets – or maybe it would, who knows, people buy some crazy crap now, I mean, people wear crocs!!!

TIP: When choosing your business name, have a look at 123reg.co.uk and make sure the domain name that you would want is available, too. You might have an awesome name, but if you can't get the domain name for it, then it's going to be difficult when you come to creating a website, building sales funnels or getting a professional email.

Another thing to check is companies house (in the UK). This is where you will go to register your business and to set things up for your tax. I would recommend setting up as a Ltd company - mainly because of the reduced liability should anything go wrong, although you shouldn't be going into your business with a focus on failing anyway, but it's always better to be protected - but many people will operate as a sole trader. I'm no professional in this area so I would recommend you speak to an accountant or other professional regarding tax and registration type before making any decisions.

There is so much more to this section, but I want to keep it simple for now. If you would like more help on naming your business, please feel free to contact me, I'd be more than happy to help, and if you want help or guidance around the legal stuff, I'd recommend speaking to an accountant, or even another business owner.

You may even be able to reach out to someone who is doing what you want to do – try to get someone in a different area, though, so they aren't in direct competition with you.

Your Elevator Pitch

Eventually you're going to have to make some cold calls, send some emails, connect with prospects on social media or meet face to face in order to generate some business; this is where you are going to need an elevator pitch.

The idea of the elevator pitch is to outline exactly what you do and why they should consider doing business with you as opposed to your competitors, in just a few short sentences – effectively in the time that it takes to travel from the ground floor to the top floor in a tall city building elevator (this is where the big-wigs with the cheque books have their offices).

Focus on what it is that the listener will want to hear, think about their business goals, the things that they may be having difficulty with, and the process that you go through to guarantee success.

I've included an example below to give you an idea of the sort of thing you should be aiming for, but make it personal to you, and include the parts that make you and your business unique.

I help people who want to achieve massive results in their business through marketing, content and a great brand; I help them break down their business goals into simple, actionable steps that are easy to follow, and I keep them on track until they've achieved the results they're looking for.

Try writing yours below.

How do you do it?

So, you've captured their attention – great news! But now you need to explain exactly how this amazing work that you do happens.

My advice is to keep it simple, highlight the main steps that you take and ensure you include the outcome that they should expect. It's important to sell the dream, describe exactly what success will look like with you.

Have a look at the example below and build yours around this template.

"It depends on the business. I look at the business's goals, the challenges that they are facing, and the opportunities they might be missing. I also uncover any hidden problems that may be sabotaging their desired results.

Then I create an action plan and we implement it together so that they finally get the results they have been looking for, but were unable to find - and of course, we address challenges that come up along the way.

The best way for me to assess all of this is to have one of my 'Make more money with marketing, 30 minute sessions', during which we create a crystal clear vision for ultimate success, uncover hidden challenges that may be standing in your way, and you'll leave the session feeling renewed, re-energized and inspired to get the results faster and easier than ever before (or than you thought possible).

If you are looking to grow your business, this might be a great place for you to start.

I'd be happy to offer that to you, on the house. This is something that people normally pay £100 for but I'd be happy to offer it with my compliments this time."

Create yours below.

....
....
....
....
....
....
....
....
....
....
....
....
....
....
....
....
....
....
....

Preparing for this is a great way to ensure that when an opportunity arises, you are ready to speak with confidence.

This is one fact that many people overlook; being prepared will make your more confident. Most anxiety around speaking comes from not being sure of the what you are about to say, or the information that you are giving.

Prepare yourself and speak so confidently that they'll have no option but to say yes to you.

Part Five

MAKING YOUR BUSINESS SOCIAL

Social Media Platforms

Social media is evolving at a rate that even the world's greatest marketers are struggling to keep up with and it's only going to continue. Each platform is flooded with thousands of pieces of content being posted every second, but that shouldn't stop you from getting a piece of the action.

Don't make the mistake of attempting to be on every platform, it's simply not manageable – especially not this early on if you're a one-person-business.

What you should focus on here is understanding what each platform is good for, and how it will add value to your business.

Consider what type of content works best for you, if you are unsure, test them out. Try product photos, infographics, pictures of your product or service in use, social events, blogs, vlogs, audios, slide shows, testimonials and presentations; whatever it is that you want to produce, see what works best, and on which platform you see the most engagement.

Once you have established which platform is good for a specific content type, build those platforms into your social strategy.

Let's focus on doubling, tripling, or even 10Xing your presence on social media.

Facebook Advertising

Facebook advertising is a must for most business, both B2B and B2C, but especially for B2C organisations.

Facebook has made it much more of a challenge to promote your business through paid ads, and you must play to their rules to get the best result.

I'm not going to go into detail about this as it would be a book in itself, plus it changes so often that it would be out of date within a month.

Facebook advertising is a great way to boost your social following and awareness of your brand. Every business I have ever been involved in has seen huge benefits from using Facebook, both in terms of audience growth and sales through advertising.

Since Facebook bought Instagram, it's now easy for your ads to appear on both Facebook and Instagram, so if you have a visual product, I'd recommend building a presence on both of these sites.

It's easy to waste money on Facebook advertising, however, it is often about testing, measuring and adjusting, to find out what works best for your business.

The first step is understanding exactly what it is that you want to achieve.

Take a clean sheet of paper and write down the things that you want to achieve using Facebook advertising.

From that list, what is the number one item that you want to achieve? Write it down.

Now… throw that piece of paper away – it means nothing!

What you want is **sales.**

Everyone should be focusing on generating sales. This is the number one goal for you with Facebook ads. Sales.

To put it simply, social media is just media exposure, or what I like to call 'digital word of mouth'. Keep focused on getting more exposure, reaching more people, engaging your audience to get them to give you their details, and to end up converting those details into actionable leads, and finally sales.

In the past, my clients paid me for coming up with the ideas that would get them to a sale, and for the execution of the plan. I followed 5 key steps to get the results that I needed for my clients, and you can follow the same 5 steps for your business in order to try and see similar levels of success. If you would like further help on this, please refer to the back of this book where my contact details are listed.

The 5 tips to delivering results, quickly

1. **Know your niche... become an expert**

You need to know your niche well, and if you haven't defined your niche, then it's important that you do this sooner rather than later, in fact, you should do it before you go any further forward.

You need to become an expert in that niche, so I recommend subscribing to magazines, signing up to websites, buying relevant books, and reading as many eBooks and online articles as you can; you must become an expert for your business to work.

However, as Russell Brunson (the Click Funnels dude) says, you are the expert of your own life. Nobody has experienced a life that is the same as yours. People may have experienced a similar life, but never the same. So, you have knowledge and life experience that could help someone else. This is what you will capitalise on when starting your business - your own individual experience.

2. **Focus on the end result – the goal.**

You need to put all your time and effort into marketing that will help you to get the result that you want. Every single thing that you do, every article that you write, every picture that you take and every post that you create should be geared towards achieving your end goal

– if it isn't, you need to consider if you need to be doing it.

In the first instance, it's likely that you will need to run some A/B tests, even try a few different content types out, as well as working out your tone and style. Constantly testing everything that you do is what will help you to deliver the results you want.

You can't improve what you can't measure.

3. **Ensure that you can stick to your strategy.**

In the same way that you would always plan a journey from one location to another, your marketing efforts must also be planned in the same way.

Before you start, you need to create a strategy and a content plan that aligns with the goals that you want to achieve. You must start with the end goal in mind and then work backwards, deciding what the smaller goals are that must be achieved first.

I like to think of this strategy like a cooking recipe; each step must be followed in a specific order, and failing to include a step, or mixing the order up will deliver an undesired result.

Imagine buttering your bread before putting it in the toaster, the result wouldn't be the same.

4.   Understand the social landscape.

You don't need to be an expert on social media marketing strategies, but you certainly need to stay up to date with what works and what doesn't, along with any changes to the algorithms that could affect your efforts. There are loads of ways to do this, such as buying courses, reading books, looking at whitepapers, downloading eBooks. You need to be as up to date as possible.

I know what you're thinking, how can I do all of this?

Well, if you can't learn it, or you don't have the time to learn it, then find someone who can do it for you. I've worked with a range of organisations, both established and start-ups, to develop a social media strategy that delivers results, but it requires consistency and commitment over a long period of time – are you up for that?

If you'd like to learn more about my social media coaching or social media services, contact me using the details at the end of the book.

However, if money isn't available right now, I'd suggest focusing on 1 social media channel, learning everything you can about it, and maximise your advertising exposure.

One way that people supercharge their social media reach is by working with an influencer who is not in direct competition with them, but already has an audience of people like those that they are trying to reach.

Another way to maximise your results is to partner up with a company who target the same audience as you, but aren't in direct competition, I call these *complimentary organisations*. An example of this would be a wedding cake maker partnering with a wedding venue. I won't go into detail about this now, but if you would like more information, again, use the details at the end of this book and I'll be happy to help.

TIP: When I first started out approaching businesses, I was nervous, anxious, lacked any real sales capability, was uncertain of my own ability, and I even questioned why someone would pay me to do this when there are hundreds, if not thousands, of people more experienced than me at doing this.

Since you're reading this book, I'm sure the thought has crossed your mind, maybe you're feeling this way with your business, or perhaps you've felt it in the past?

What you must remember is that people don't know what they don't know. The local dentist that you want to offer social media services to, in order to bring in more private clients for cosmetic dentistry, may not be aware that you can use Facebook for advertising, they may not realise that you can manage an advertising budget with ease or, if they did know about Facebook advertising, they may expect that it's going to cost them thousands of pounds upfront in order to see a result.

What you must do is inform them, give them the information, explain what it is that you do, and then see if they are interested. You're simply educating someone on what is available and, if they're not interested, perhaps they know someone who is – always ask this!

If you're still feeling anxious about this or have a sinking feeling of self-doubt and impending rejection, then you should consider this trick that I still use today.

Think of your calls or emails as helping someone rather than selling to someone – which I know salespeople have a bad reputation for at times – because we all love to help people, and helping people makes us feel good.

Changing the way I thought about my sales efforts really helped me to be more confident on the phone. I even took it a step further and, should someone say no to me on the phone, I offered a free eBook to them that introduced them to some simple aspects of what I wanted to help them with – so, I still managed to get their email address and add them into my mailing list... and guess what, many of those people became customers shortly after.

5.   **Master Facebook/ Instagram advertising as quickly as you can.**

You must become an expert in Facebook advertising. The reason I have chosen Facebook is that it has, in my opinion, the most advanced and targeted advertising capability of all of the available social platform (although since writing this, YouTube has greatly risen along with

Instagram), plus, it now includes Instagram with its advertising – and Instagram is widely being highlighted at the social channel to be mastering for 2019.

I've often said that;

People love to write the words, but don't want to read the numbers.

Analytics are what will guide your strategy and allow you to assess, adjust and improve.

You must appreciate the numbers involved in each and every campaign, without doing this, you are leaving your results to chance – you can't improve what you can't measure (you'll come to see that I love this quote).

Three advertising strategies for success

When I first launched myself into the world of social media with the intention of promoting what it was that I wanted to do – help people with anxiety and self-doubt to start a passion-filled business, or to accelerate an existing but stagnant business, so that they can live life to its fullest – the thing that held me back most, was knowing what to say or what to write.

I was so anxious about the fact that I might end up waffling or not making any sense, that I'd just not post anything. I was paralysed by the very thing that I was trying to help people to overcome!

Thankfully, after a long time, a lot of research, trial and error, and focus, I no longer have this problem! Unfortunately, this can't be fixed with a magic tablet or the flick of a switch, this must be solved with hard work – buy you're up for this, right?

The way to solve this issue, is to know what options you have, what works, and when it works. So, to make this easy for you, so that you don't have to go through what I went through trying to work it all out, I've explained some of the best principles and content types that you should use when creating value to your audience.

It will be hard at first but, trust me, it will get easier once you begin.

Story Telling

One thing I know for sure is that people love stories. Whether it's telling them, hearing them, or making them up as excuses, we all love a good story – it's human nature and has been engrained in us all since we were children.

But how does this help you to sell? I'll explain from a psychological point of view. Humans have and always will make most decisions based on emotion, combined with a little bit of logic, with the primary focus of either finding pleasure or avoiding pain.

An example of this would be when someone takes their hands off the steering wheel and covers their eyes just before they have a crash – yes, I have witnessed this as a passenger!

If you ask the driver, why they let go of the steering wheel and effectively removed their ability to see during this crucial moment, they will say something along the lines of, "I just panicked" – which not only proves my point that emotion is the stronger of the emotions in the decision making process, but also that emotion can make you do things that you know you should not be doing!

Crazy, right!?

Well, the world of marketing has made a shift from simply pushing a product based on features alone (because this is a purely logic-based approach, and we know people don't buy on this), or even its attractive price (logic again), to building a strong and long-lasting connection with the audience through the use of emotion-invoking words, or stories.

You must talk about the *why* and share this though your adverts on Facebook; think about the purpose of the story and understand exactly what it is that you are trying to achieve.

If you have a camera, or the money to have a video created professionally, I would fully recommend that you consider a video to promote your offering. Literally anything can be sold through video, and this is because you're going to be selling the story, the pain, the feelings, the emotion, you're going to be selling on the outcome and what that does for the buyer.

Example

An example of this is a video advert showing a beautiful vehicle, a 4x4, driving through tough terrain with the driver smiling, his wife in the front looking equally happy, and his two beautiful children in the back; one playing with a toy and the youngest fast asleep. They come to a stop at the top of a large rocky hill and the parents step out of the vehicle, the child playing with the toy runs around happily, and the youngest remains asleep in the arms of the mother. From the towering cliffside, they look out to the ocean and the father looks at his family with content. He places his arm around his wife as the screen fades to black with large white text that appears saying, "Adventure is for sharing..." and the vehicle logo appears underneath.

This advert is completely fictional, but I'm sure something similar has been used many times before. In this example, there is no mention of the number of gears, the type of seat material, air con, sound system, or anything that would help to make a logical decision. In fact, you're not really buying the car, you're buying the story, the emotion - you're buying the feeling. This is what will help you to sell. People want to see themselves in the advert, they want to imagine what their life will be like if they bought that product.

Another great example of this is Dollar Shave Club. I'm in love with this company and, although I've never purchased from them, I do admire their marketing and I have shared it with several hundreds of people.

I'm not going to go into detail about their video advert, but it's nothing short of hilarious – again, selling on emotion.

The idea is that you buy into the comical side of the brand first, and then you come to see that it would be much simpler to have shaving equipment delivered to you, rather than risking running out of blades when you need a shave for that important meeting at work. I'd recommend having a look at their video on YouTube, it's pretty awesome.

Facebook Offers

Think about a time that you were considering a purchase but had doubts about going through with it. Those doubts might have been around cost or even uncertainty as to whether you need it the product; but then something magical happens... you see that very same product... ON OFFER! And this changes everything.

When you see that it's on offer or at a discounted rate for short period of time you make the decision and go through with the purchase.

This is a great tactic that people use to create urgency. As humans, when we believe that something is limited or scarce, its perceived value increases and the risk of 'missing out' becomes more of a concern to us than whether or not we really need it – and so we pull out our wallets and pay.

Have I not convinced you that this is a great way to promote your product, yet? No? OK, what about this? Think about a time that you were in town looking for a particular item, but then you see a product on sale; it's not the product you were in town for, in fact you had no intention of buying this product, but the price caused you to make the purchase. Maybe you felt that it was a good deal that you couldn't miss out on?

This is the power of offers, or discounts. Promoting an offer is a great way to attract new customers and to encourage them to take action.

Email Marketing

Yes, email marketing.

I know what you're thinking – "but you said this is about social media and email isn't social media!"

Yes, I did, and I know that email marketing isn't social media, but using Facebook and other paid social channels to gather emails is a great way to improve the delivery of your message.

Growing your email list allows you to control and improve the level of engagement that your content receives. Using only Facebook to deliver your message means that Facebook's algorithm decides who sees your content.

Recent changes have meant that Facebook is more geared toward promoting friend and family content as opposed to business content, unless you pay using ads like we discussed above. Using Facebook, coupled with Facebook ads, to build an email list gives you the control to decide who receives your message and when.

TIP - Remember that you don't always have to be selling via social media. One really effective way to market is to engage and educate people via social media and sell via email. You'll do well to remember that.

Building your brand with Twitter – 10 content types for success

Building your personal or business brand on any social platform is no easy task and this is no different for Twitter. If anything, it can actually be a lot harder, what with the pure mass of content that is shared on a daily basis by its users, and also the 'like, in hope of a follow' approach that many Twitter users put into action.

The key with Twitter is to post consistently over a long period of time, with a varied range of content types that include personal content, images, links and other people's content.

Creating content can be difficult, especially when many Twitter users post anywhere from 1 to 50+ times a day; so how do you keep producing relevant but varied content on mass?

TIP – Until recently, many Twitter users were using auto posters to recycle posts that would give the impression of heavy activity. Twitter has since released an update that prevents the same post being issued twice. There are ways around this, but I'm raising this to make you aware that posting a couple of times a day is very much acceptable; don't try to compete with those posting 20+ times a day.

I'm going to get you going on Twitter by sharing 10 different content types that you can take advantage of when creating your content strategy for Twitter.

1. **Word/ quote images**

Whenever you come across a quote or section from a book that you feel would be valued by your target audience, share it via Twitter with a link to the book or tagging in the account that the quote originated from.

Additionally, you could use the quote to create an image and then share it via Twitter (image-based tweets are engaged with more often than text tweets).

2. **Blogs**

If you have a blog that you post to regularly, share the content with your audience by sharing the link, perhaps a small section of text and an eye-catching image.

3. **Giveaways**

If you produce eBooks or educational content that your audience will find to be of value, share the link to this content via your Twitter page and encourage people to share the link with their followers.

An additional tip would be to update your Twitter bio with the link to your latest giveaway to increase the level of engagement with it.

4. **Other people's content**

Sharing other people's content will not only get you noticed by the content creator, but other users will begin to see you as a great source of content; with you doing all of the leg work to find and share such great information, they can use you as their primary source of knowledge, rather than spending the time sourcing it themselves.

5. **Personal Tweets**

People like to see behind the curtain, we're nosey, we want to see how the 'other half' live – so share some of your behind the scenes content.

This could be you at home, in the office, at a factory having something created, out at lunch, on holiday – literally anything.

When you do this, let your personality shine through. If you're a joker, share something that you find funny or something that you have created that you find funny. If you're serious, share something educational that will benefit your followers. The chances are that your followers will have similar interests to you and, as a result, are likely to enjoy similar content to you.

6. **Motivational Tweets**

No matter what your Twitter page's focus is, there will always be a relevant way to motivate your audience. Whether through sharing a story, an achievement, an image or someone else's story, there will always be a way to motivate your audience. Just try to make sure it is relevant and consistent with your brand.

7. **Published Content**

If you write or create content for other mediums, such a press, magazines or as a contributor for someone else's blog, make sure you share the direct link with your Twitter audience. Not only will this promote your content further, but it will increase your chance of capturing an additional audience and promote you as a worthy contributor.

8. **Top Tips**

Everyone loves to learn something new and there is no better way to capture new knowledge than in bitesize paragraphs that are simple and to the point.

9. **Video**

If you produce video content, have your own vlog or value the video content of someone else, sharing video is a great way to deliver a message and portray your knowledge and personality at the same time.

You can also screen and voice record a PowerPoint presentation and turn that into a video or an audiobook for people who prefer to listen or watch their content, rather than reading.

10. **Slideshare**

When creating presentations on PowerPoint or other presentation platforms, why not see if you can edit it slightly to create a presentation that will be a value-add to your Twitter audience. Short presentations are a great way to share content, findings, and graphics in a single location.

What's next with Twitter?

Posting content is a great way to get noticed on Twitter, but you're going to want to connect with specific, relevant people that you find yourself, in addition to those that come across your content, so what's the best way to do this?

There are several ways to attract the attention of specific people on Twitter, but I am going to share the two that I most commonly use:

Method 1

Search for keywords and phrases that are relevant to your business. For example, if I was a driving instructor, I might search for people who have posted "can anyone recommend a driving instructor" or "I want to learn to drive".

You're probably wondering how I would sift through the thousands of tweets from people, plus those in other countries, and just highlight those from people in my area.

You can google "twitter advanced search" or just go to this link (www.twitter.com/search-advanced) and change the location to UK, or Leicester, or wherever it is that you cover. You can also get really smart and think outside of the box, for example, I know that the legal age for driving in the UK is 17, so I could search for people who are celebrating their 17th birthday by using terms such as: "17 years old today" or "happy 17th birthday"; this could be a great way of attracting those who are the perfect audience for your product.

Method 2

The next method is to search for companies or pages that are complimentary to your business, but not in competition.

An example of this would be a wedding photographer and a complimentary business would be a wedding cake maker, or a wedding dress shop. You search for these pages and then go through their contacts and connect with those people that follow them. It's that simple.

Top tips for guaranteed Instagram growth

Whatever industry you are in, you need to build your own personal brand. Instagram is one of the best channels for you to promote your brand visually and to harness your audience. They have over 500 million daily active users and, with a huge range of industries, this is the perfect place for you to start.

I have only recently started to realise the potential of Instagram and have already seen amazing results in terms of followers, engagement and sales.

Below I have outlined 5 key tips to setting yourself up for success with Instagram.

1. **Utilise your bio space.**
Explain in simple words why someone should follow you. This usually means saying what result they will get from you, followed by how you do it. I'd advise against hashtags in your bio unless it is a hashtag that you have created and only really used in relation to your brand.

If you stuff hashtags into your bio, page visitors may be tempted to click the hashtag (they act as links) and then be taken to a page filled with thousands of images from other people using the same hashtag, and you've lost your potential follower or customer.

You also have space to include a single link in your bio section. The aim here is for you to take the viewer from your Instagram page to your website or other desired location, such as a landing page – so make sure you have the link included in your bio description.

Nearly 100% of Instagram users are viewing this link on their phone, so this is where you must make sure you have a mobile-optimised site because it is likely that this is how they are going to be viewing your site. If you don't do this, then you are going to lose the visitor which will waste all the work that you have done with your Instagram page.

Also, make sure that your brand on Instagram aligns with your brand on your website. Failure to do this can cause confusion and cause the viewer to leave your site.

TIP - A top tip is to send people to a specific product or service page or send them to a page where only one specific action is required. If you give the visitor too many options, they make not make any decision at all. Sales funnels are a great option for your bio link.

Alternatively, you can use a website like link tree, whereby you can add a couple of links that direct the visitor to different product options. This is a free site, although there is a paid version, and it's great for listing multiple sites or for sharing your other social profiles.

2. **Create an awesome content strategy.**
Whatever it is you post, make sure you post regularly. I would recommend that you post every single day, at least once. NEVER miss a day of posting, especially when you are starting out.

You don't have to post quotes like many people do on Instagram, just focus on what will resonate with your audience. Think about what your audience will find to be valuable and stick to posting that form of content.

You can also consider using social proof if you have a physical product, by posting photos of people with your product or using your service you can attract new customers and reassure them that your product is a worthy purchase; but make sure the photos are good quality or abstract. Instagram is visual so you need to make sure that your images stand out. Blurry or pixelated images will lose you followers, and quickly.

3. **Tools to use.**
If you want to add writing to your images, then you can do this easily. There are phone apps like Wordswag or Typorama that you can use on an apple device, or you could use Phonto which is available for Android and iOS. Canva is great for use on desktop or their new app, which is amazing for creating images that have the appearance of being professionally designed. Canva allows you to use

your own images, but they also have a huge selection of free to use stock images.

All of these are really simple to use and will help you to create great images that your audience will love. My advice is to try and be creative with your images; use different angles, fun concepts and behind the scene shots that your audience might not normally get to see.

Another site that you can also use is ink361.com to run scans on your competitors accounts so that you can see the most engaged and most liked images, and then use this information to guide you with what sort of images you should use moving forward.

TIP - People don't like to make decisions by themselves, they like to be influenced or 'nudged'. They won't click on your link in your bio unless you ask them to, so make sure you add that information in the description section of each image. I also personally found that using the pointing finger down emoji in the bio description towards my link increased the conversion rate.

4.   Using hashtags.

Hashtags are important on Instagram, so you should always post hashtags that are relevant to your image and are also related to your niche. You can use up to 30 hashtags for each picture, but my advice is to add your hashtags in the comment section under your image rather than blasting them all over your image description. I've found that using around 11 works best for me. You should also engage other accounts on Instagram who use similar hashtags to the ones that you use by liking and commenting on their images – this will help you to start to organically collect targeted followers.

TIP – If it looks like you have used a lot of hashtags in a post, double check how many you have used by counting them. The reason you should do this is that posting more than 30 hashtags will wipe the entire text field when you post your image and you will have to go back and edit the image, re-type everything from scratch, and then post it again.

5. **Engaging through shout-outs and influencers.**
One of the quickest ways to grow your account is through shout-outs and influencer promotions. You need to get as many people on Instagram to engage with your content, so they either need to like, share or comment on your posts.

There are 2 ways to do this;

The first way to do this is that you can add questions on your images requesting that people tag their friends into your comments section if they are relevant to your image (example – Tag someone who is going to be successful), you can also do this in the description section of your posts – but do it on the first line, otherwise it might get missed.

The second way is that you pay for influencers to promote your content for you to their existing fan base. Use these techniques as much as you can as they will really help you to blow-up your audience. One example of doing this is to send an influencer your product for free and get them to share a photo whilst tagging you in it and sharing your website, product, or sales funnel link.

As an idea as to what you should be paying or charging for an influencer shout-out, consider that anything less than 100,000 followers should be around £20 for 3 posts, and anything above 1,000,000 followers should be around £300 for 3 posts. This can vary depending on the cost of your product and the value that this could bring to you, but just work on negotiating with them to get a rate that works for you.

One thing you can always ask for, which may cost you more, is for the influencer to change the link in their bio to your landing page or sales funnel link. I have found this to massively increase my conversions, so it's well worth asking.

TIP - Do your due diligence and check out the account before sending any products out. There are plenty of scam artists with bought followers who are just looking for free stuff – it's a confidence knock and a cost that you don't need to deal with.

6. **Make sure you measure everything with analytics.**
You don't know what you don't measure, and you can't improve what you can't count, so make sure you are always tracking the most engaged images, the speed of your audience growth, test shout-outs of both paid an unpaid, and tracking the links in your bio because this is how you are going to get more followers, more growth and, ultimately, more money.

Some of the tools that you can use to track and measure this are the following:

Iconosquare.com – Find out engagement
Socialblade.com – Track growth
Socialrank.com – Find your most engaged followers

Additional bonus
A bonus tip, for those willing to push themselves out of their comfort zone, is to go live on Instagram. The benefit to going live on Instagram is that anyone who follows your page that is online when you go live, will receive a notification to say that you have gone live. This massively increases your engagement rate and gets your content in front of more people.

Part Six

BLOG LIKE A PRO – FOR BEGINNERS

I'm a firm believer that every business needs to create content in some form or another, whether it's an email, a book, a whitepaper, a report, eBook, or simply a letter; at some point, you are going to need to create content for your business.

Creating Killer Content

Creating content is easy; I don't care who you are, what job you do, how educated you are, or even if you have written number one best-sellers in the past, nobody will be able to convince me otherwise. It's a fact. Content can be created with ease, at speed, and in ample amounts with minimal effort.

Now, if you want to talk to me about creating quality, engaging and thought-provoking content, now that's a different story altogether.

Whether it's an email, a blog or a book that you are writing, there is a formula that I follow religiously to create killer content that guarantees maximum engagement.

The main factor that gets your reader engaged is, as we discussed earlier in this book, emotion. Emotion drives engagement. When your reader becomes emotionally attached to your content, they start to imagine themselves in the situation that you are talking about, your words become personal to them, the problems that you describe become pains that they can relate to.

So how do you get the reader to become emotionally engaged with your content?

I follow a simple 3 step process.

Step 1 – Whatever the subject of your content, work out the pain or problem that you plan to address and then give the pain or the problem a name.

Step 2 – Now that you have the name of the pain or problem that you are to address, describe what that means. Keep it short and simple but expand on what the name suggests, ensuring the reader understands.

Step 3 – What effect does the problem or pain have on those exposed to it? Explain in detail the depth of the effects that this pain or problem has on the reader – how far does the problem or pain go?

I'll show you what this would look like by using the example of writing a blog for a business to raise awareness of a product or service:

Pain/ Problem Name: Writer's block

Pain/ Problem Meaning: The inability to effectively engage a target audience through lack of inspiration or content ideas

Pain/ Problem Effects: Failing to create engaging and inspiring content for your product, through lack of ideas, effectively stalls the promotion of your product and your revenue generation. This can also lead to sub-standard content being released that not only fails to convert prospects into customers but turns them off your brand, completely.

Once you have established these 3 areas, you are now in the perfect position to start structuring your content.

My advice here is to flip these 3 rules on their head when starting your content.

Use the EFFECTS section to create your title or email subject line, for example, 'Is writer's block damaging your brand?'

When starting the body text of your content, continue with the effects section, for example, '70% of start-up businesses said that even if they knew their content was poor due to lack of ideas or inspiration, they would still publish content in order to remain present for their followers with 40% of those start-ups admitting that they believed they had lost followers and maybe even customers as a result of poor or boring content...'

Now introduce the MEANING stage, for example, 'Is the inability to create great content on a regular basis negatively affecting your brand?'

Followed by the NAME stage, for example, 'Download this free eBook on overcoming Writer's Block for start-ups'

This is a technique that I have used for several years and has been proven to develop emotion, generate interest and, ultimately, build lists, provide leads and make sales.

Part Seven

EMAIL MASTERY

Creating Emails with Higher Open Rates

By now your confidence with content creation should be starting to grow, so moving into email should be a breeze and, if you have been building your email list as we explained in part 5, you will be in a good position to start reaching out to those prospects.

Having a great message or a mouth-watering offer is one of the best ways to engage your prospect customers through email marketing, I mean, come on, who doesn't want great content and big discounts straight to their phone?

However, there's a hurdle that often gets overlooked. How do you get the recipient to open the email in the first place? This problem is much bigger if the recipient hasn't engaged with you via email before.

However, the answer is simple. Use the subject line.

The subject line is the little box where your creativity needs to excel. You need to use very few words to grab the recipient's attention and generate interest – if you fail to do this, your email is just another piece of junk mail that's about to get deleted or, worse, unsubscribed from.

My advice is this, "STOP BEING BORING! START YOUR EMAIL MORE EFFECTIVELY".

That's easier said than done, you might be thinking?

Below, I have shared some example ideas for your subject lines that will seem personal, interesting and worthy of at least an open.

- "I loved your post (or tweet) on X."
- "I'm hoping to get your insight on X."
- "I want to share an idea that addresses [pain point]."
- "Is X a priority for you right now?"
- "Did you know [interesting fact]?"
- "What do you think about [specific industry event or news piece]?"
- "Yesterday, you did X. Any particular reason?"
- "I noticed your company recently …"

Using these subject lines, amongst a whole host of others that you can come up with, will help you to capture the recipient's attention directly from their inbox.

You will stand yourself head and shoulders above the other boring mail that they receive, and even some of the mail that they look forward to receiving.

20 creative ways to get people to respond to your email

Many people think that making cold calls is scary, but sending emails can be scary, too.

Imagine you've gone to a networking event and arrived on your own and walked into the room full of people who just seemed to ignore you; it's not very likely that you will start trying to sell your product or service to them.

Sending prospective emails can sometimes feel a bit like this – you create what you believe is great content and send it to your mailing list and then, nothing – and this happens to you over and over again. This is often down to the message itself, but it can also be down to the way that you are building your mailing list.

So, let's assume you are writing an email to a new contact and your aim is to try and build interest – this person knows very little about you and they certainly won't know if what you offer can help them – what's the next step?

I get hundreds of emails every week with people trying to sell me products or services, inviting me to attend a random event, or simply trying to schedule a time for a call with me; I'll be honest, most of them get deleted.

It's not because I'm trying to be rude, I simply don't have the time to reply to all of them. However, every now and then I get an email that captures my attention, causes me to spend the time reading its content, and I even reply!

Do you know what the difference is? CREATIVITY!

When I come across something that grabs my attention and has something a little "wow" about it, I'm intrigued to learn more.

I wanted to share some ideas for what I do to capture the attention of new contacts.

1. Send a video, or link to an audio file, to introduce yourself and your services and explain how you can help them specifically
2. Send an invitation to a webinar event that focuses on pains specific to their sector
3. Create a presentation, and host it online, that talks specifically about how your business could help or collaborate with theirs
4. Send an email that mentions competitors of theirs you are working with and explain the benefits they have seen since working with you
5. Create an email that comments on an article in the media that they have recently published and request more information or add further value
6. Send an email that talks about industry specific events or news that they will need to know about
7. Invite them to attend an event with you and provide a ticket (even if the event is free)
8. Add a comment to an article or blog post and then follow up with an email for more information about that article

9. Explain that you are looking to write an article for a specialist magazine and that you would like to add comment from someone in their position
10. Invite them to be interviewed or included in a podcast
11. Send over an eBook that you have recently created
12. Send a message on their birthday
13. Offer to provide a free report or analysis on some part of their business for them
14. Send a PDF of your book and ask them for their feedback
15. Send them an invitation to a podcast that you are hosting or speaking on
16. Send them a link to a social post or image that you have recently created
17. Send an InMail on LinkedIn that explains the value of you connecting without trying to sell
18. Create a social post and tag them in it, then follow up with an email
19. Offer to collaborate on some content together
20. Invite them to a group that you manage on social media

There are so many ways to engage with a new prospect that doesn't involve trying to sell.

Trust me, if you can keep it together for just a few exchanges of conversation, you will literally 10X your conversion rates!

Part Eight
SUCCESS LOGGING

Why it's Important to Write it Down

I wasn't going to cover Success Logging in this book, however, throughout the process of writing it, I came to find that my Success Log actually helped me to finish writing the book, set life and business goals with deadlines, and even jogged my memory with bits of information about things that I had overlooked or had slipped my mind.

In short, a Success Log is a bit like a diary or a journal – but not the *Dear Diary* type of diary – it's a journal created specifically for entrepreneurs and those that want more out of their life.

The idea is to write down key goals, lessons, successes and aspirations that you have for a 12 month period, usually from January 1st to December 31^{st,} although there is a physical version of the Success Log that you can now purchase which allows you to start you Success Log from any day of the year and run it for a 365 day period.

I first started Success Logging 4 or 5 years ago, but I've been doing it in the way that I do now for around 2 years – if you stick to it, it truly is a game changer.

You see, I'm all for setting goals, and would wholeheartedly suggest that you create and write down your goals, otherwise, chances are, you'll fail – or the goal will shrink or change to avoid you failing – in essence, still a failure. But, when I was told that you should write down your goals every day for them to materialise, even twice a day some people suggest, I wasn't sure about it.

I tried this approach for around 6 months and, yes, for the first month or so, I enjoyed writing out my goals, watching them alter and grow, and seeing new goals add to my list. But, after a short while, it became monotonous and boring; I started to short-hand my goals and miss words out to get it done quicker, it became a chore – and I didn't want to associate my goals with being a chore.

So, I looked for another way to track my goals and record my personal growth, because I saw the value in writing things down, I just didn't like the way that most entrepreneurs were suggesting I should do it.

This is when I came across a guy called Clarke Kegley, on YouTube. Clarke is an awesome guy who has some great videos on Journaling, but I wasn't 100% set on doing things the way that Clarke taught, either. So, I decided to create my own way of doing things.

By combining bits from other entrepreneurs with some bits from Clarke, I devised what I believe to be, and am going to claim IS IN FACT, the best way to map, monitor and achieve your goals... I present to you, SUCCESS LOGGING.

I won't go into every detail of the Success Log; however, I'll give you a list of 10 key points for you to get started.

1.   Your Success Log can be any size. Initially, I chose an A4, 1 page per day, diary. I got it from Tesco, and it

cost me around £2.99. This is really all you need to get started. Since then, I have created a physical Success Log that I now use, and they are available for you to buy. There is a video course with tons of bonus material and worksheets that you can also get to supplement the Success Log and your growth. You can get free access to the start of the first module of the video course if you visit the website below.

https://empire-consulting-group.com/free-access

The next few points about the Success Log are written with the assumption that you are using a blank, page-per-day diary.

2. On the inside left-hand page, you need to write down how your life is today, the way things are for you right now.

You can include things such as your current job title, your current salary, how much debt you have, how many credit cards you have, where you live, who you live with, are you single, married or divorced, how much do you weigh, how would you describe your physique or your general fitness and health, and how old you are.

One powerful thing to do on this page is the following – assume that you are going to live until you are 90 (at least), how many days do you have left until you are 90 years old? This really helps to put into perspective exactly how much time we really have on this planet. You may be surprised.

3.	The inside right-hand page is to write down how you want your life to be, along with quotes and sayings that you are going to live by for the next 12 months, at least.

So, you can state what your job status will be, what you want to be earning, where you will live, what your relationship status will be, what education you will have gained, and what your mantra is going to be.

4.	Now, go to the back of your Success Log. The inside left- and right-hand pages are for writing down and tracking your goals. I recommend breaking your goals down into three areas.

The areas are as follows;

Growth and Contribution: this is where you write down goals related to business, education, and progression of your business potential.

Health and Mind: this is where you write down goals about your finances, your physical health and appearance, and your mind.

Fun and Adventure: this is the section where you write down goals on trips you want to go away on, experiences you want to have, and even things that you want to buy that have a positive impact on you or that act as a reward.

5. You write on the page that aligns with the day of the year that it is. So, if it's the 3rd of November, you write on the page that is the 3rd of November – simple. When writing on a page, try to use a mixture of red, black and blue pens to highlight different things – plus using arrows and bubbles is encouraged!

6. You DO NOT have to write in your Success Log every day. You only write when you want to write, or if you feel that you have something to record.

7. If you want to record some information or create a checklist that you may refer to in the future, but you have already used the page for that day, go back to a page in the past when you didn't write anything, don't skip ahead and use pages in the future.

8. I recommend to everyone that I work with that reading is so important to personal growth, and the many lessons that you will learn from reading should be recorded in your Success Log. So, when you read a book and you learn something that you want to refer to or remember, write it in your Success Log.

9. At the beginning of your Success Log, it doesn't have to be January the 1st, but sometime early into your

Success Logging journey, use one of your pages to write about The Power of 'I AM'. This has been truly powerful on my journey and has also been a great reminder that I could flick back to it when I needed to.

The Power of 'I AM' section should list your most important goals and aspirations as if they have already happened. This should help you to visualise them and, eventually, have them materialise.

Here's a quick example: I am the owner of a beautiful, black-gated, 4-bedroom house.

And one more example: I have investments that deliver more than £2,000 in passive income every single month.

10. Use the bottom of each page to jot down content ideas. So, if you create blogs, videos or social posts, whatever it is you do, you can build up a bank of, what will eventually be, 365 content ideas – 1 for every day of the year.

In the physical copy of the Success Log, called the Elite edition, there is a 90-day challenge that guides you through a daily challenge and a live video that you are to do.

Part Nine

TOP TIPS SUMMARY

This step is key, as the steps you followed at the start of this book will now be less memorable than the ones you have read more recently. It's important to me that you have understood the lessons properly and you haven't overlooked or misunderstood a step.

I know how easy it is to take some statements as gospel rather than applying them to your own individual situation – a few years back I read from Grant Cardone that he emails his prospects every day, so, being a huge fan of the Big GC, I took to emailing HR Directors every single day to sell software to them...

Well, what a disaster it was!

Grant Cardone is selling sales courses, books, merchandise and other sales-related materials, directly to a list of prospects who can make a buying decision at any time, with no tie to a specific date or event - this makes emailing daily an acceptable process.

However, when I was selling software to HR Seniors, there was a range of factors that needed to be considered, such as sign-off procedure, renewal dates, budget etc. which made daily emails an inconvenience and even an annoyance – needless to say, I lost many subscribers with this approach.

The below points are great reminders to live by and to refer to during your journey.

1. **Marketing isn't a one-button-push exercise.**
You must exercise your strategy over a period of time whilst producing regular content and interacting with your audience on a regular basis.

2. **Be yourself.**
If you try and be someone or something that you are not, you will feel uncomfortable and that will shine through to your audience, more than likely making them feel uncomfortable, too.

3. **Marketing is more than email.**
Remember that marketing is an all-round activity, from the business card that you hand over and the website that people land on, to the tone of voice that you speak in and the images that you share on your social pages. Heck, even the colour that you wear on a regular basis can easily become a recognisable part of your brand.

4. **Live Video and Stories.**
Since the tail-end of 2017, video has been hugely prioritised by some of the biggest players in social media and that has continued into 2019.

This is one of the biggest routes in to your audience as it allows you to notify all of your followers at once that you are live and allows a constant stream of engaging content. You need to maximise this as soon as you can.

5. **Money doesn't sort out your marketing.**
Marketing is all about finding the people who get you and understand what you are trying to achieve. Your marketing aim should be to reach these people, engage with them and convert them from loyal followers into customers and even evangelists.

6. **Know who you are.**
One of the biggest mistakes that businesses make today is trying to be everything to everyone. You need to target the one type of person that is already interested in what you do. Anyone who is anyone, is anyone because they aren't trying to be everyone!

7. **Align your message with your market.**
Know what the right message is, who the right people are for that message, and which medium they are present on, and when they are most likely to find that message.

8. **Don't be a one-man band.**
Share your work load. You don't have to do everything on your own. Work with people who are great at things you aren't so good at so that you can concentrate on the things that you are good at. Being greedy gets you nowhere.

9. **Branding should be simple, yet effective.**
To start with, understand what a brand is and what you want your brand to be. Work out your brand values, stick to those values and then align everything that you do to those brand values.

10. **(KLT) Know - like - trust.**
Be trusted. Your starting point is to get your target audience to know who you are, once you become recognised, you need to ensure that what you are sharing is making your audience like you, make sure they enjoy your content.

Once you have done this, you need to establish trust with that audience, remain on-brand, stick to your tone of voice and be loyal to who you really are – this will help to achieve a strong and memorable brand.

Part Ten

USEFUL TOOLS

I have created a list of tools that helped me during my early days starting out, and many I still use today. I count this section as a necessary "step" as you should create your own list of relevant and useful tools.

With so many popping up on a pretty much weekly basis, you can easily overlook and even forget about the tools that could be making things easier for you.

Use my list as a starting point and then continue to build your own – you'll thank me for this in the future!

To be 100% open with you, some of the links below are affiliate links, so I will make a small commission if you access the service via that link. However, as a thank-you for using my affiliate link, some links do come with extra materials that I have provided to help accelerate your journey.

Creating Your Own Images

Pixlr

Canva ← This one, seriously, AMAZING!

Gimp

Picmonkey

Relaythat

Pexels ← And this one will save your £100's in images

Adazing ← Awesome for 3D eBook covers etc

Social Media Management Tools

Instagress – automate Instagram likes and followers

Hootsuite – Manage multiple social media accounts

Socialoomph – Schedule social posts via a bucket system

Recurpost – An alternative social posting bucket system (I prefer this one)

Manageflitter – Manage your Twitter account

Sproutsocial – Manage multiple social media accounts

Rival IQ – Competitor social media account analysis

Google Keyword Planner – Information around which keywords to use

Twitaholic – Twitter analytics

Twittercounter.com – Twitter stats

Trends24.in – What's trending on Twitter

Ritetag.com – Hashtags for Twitter

Hashtagify.me – The best hashtags to use on Twitter

Buzzsumo – Relevant articles being shared for a particular search term on social media

Getpocket.com – Store interesting articles quickly and access from phone or computer

Management Tools

To build simple websites for small businesses, I recommend Wix. Although it does have some down-points, for the type of traffic and functionality that a small business will require, it offers everything you will need and is easy enough to manage yourself because of its WYSIWYG (drag and drop) editor.

http://wixstats.com/?a=26691&c=2252&s1=

I use ClickFunnels to build sales funnels. Now, don't be fooled by the adverts that say how easy this is to use — yes, compared to coding a website, ClickFunnels is super easy, but the back-end set-up and learning curve is actually quite steep. Then, even if you do manage to work out how to use it, understanding the psychology of the sales content, images, layout and the whole prospect journey, that's another challenge in itself.

I have clients that I help with this, from complete creation to hand-holding and consultancy. If you decide that ClickFunnels is the way you want to go for selling your product or service, I recommend using my affiliate link as I will provide additional benefits to you that you won't get going direct to the ClickFunnels site (and you pay the same price!)

https://clickfunnels.com/?cf_affiliate_id=1419356&affiliate_id=1419356&aff_sub=dashboard&aff_sub2=trial

Popular Instagram Hashtags

#photooftheday

#WCW

#TravelTuesdays

#selfie

#instalike

#tbt / throwbackthursday

#motivationalmonday

#followfriday / ff

#instaquote

#amreading

#quoteoftheday

#amwriting

#widn (what I'm doing now)

#blogging

#newblogpost

#instablogger

Continued Learning Index

Throughout this book you will have noticed that I asked you to contact me for further information on certain areas for extra knowledge and support.

To give you easy access to these areas, I created this Continued Learning Index for you.

Email me at hello@empire-consulting.co.uk to speak about:

Accountability Partners

Online Coaching

Naming Your Company

Facebook Advertising

Understanding the Social Landscape

Twitter Strategy

Instagram Strategy

If you wish to continue learning with me, you can also find more information on products and training that I produce on the following website:

www.empire-consulting.co.uk

SUMMARY

The lessons that I have included in this book are the areas that I struggled with at first when starting out and having now spent a decade working in marketing, speaking to entrepreneurs and reading many books from many different successful people, and even embarking on my own personal journey for success, I wanted to give back and help those who are just starting out, or who have given up a number of times before and feel lost with where to turn next.

I know first-hand how hard it can be to build up the courage to even speak loudly about your dreams through fear of being mocked or humiliated, so I hope that my story can inspire you to step out from the shadows and share the greatness within you.

The supporting chapters in this book have been written to provide you with enough information to get started with your business venture, by defining your brand, your message, and your audience, you will be in a position to reach the right people, with the right message, at the right time.

Please continue to read and learn and seek further advice and guidance from someone such as a mentor as your business begins to grow.

Remember this...

"To go quickly, go alone

To go far, go together."

Here's to your success.

Thank you

Jason Staniforth

Author of The Anxious Entrepreneur

CONNECT WITH ME

I'd love to get your feedback on this book and hear about the positive changes that you see as you put the steps into practice. Use any of the links below to connect with me.

FOLLOW ME ON FACEBOOK
https://www.facebook.com/jay.staniforth

CONNECT WITH ME ON LINKEDIN
https://www.linkedin.com/in/jasonstaniforthmarketing

TWEET ME ON TWITTER
https://twitter.com/jaystaniforth

EMAIL ME DIRECTLY
hello@empire-consulting.co.uk

JOIN ME ON YOUTUBE
Jay Staniforth

FOLLOW ME ON INSTAGRAM
https://www.instagram.com/jaystaniforth/

MESSAGE ME ON SNAPCHAT
JayStaniforth87

ACKNOWLEDGEMENTS

For a long time, I have wanted to share my story, but social anxiety and fear of rejection and humiliation held me back... until now.

I've met, learnt from, laughed with, and helped, so many people since those dark and lonely days, and it's because of many of these people that I have achieved what I have today.

My Mom and Step Dad have been instrumental in everything that I have achieved, through bailing me out when money was tight, to forgiving me when mistakes were made. Without the both of you, none of what I have done in my life would have been possible.

My father, Carl, you're a wildcard in life and have shown me mostly what I should avoid, but also that I should take risks and act in spite of fear, in spite of judgement, and in search of personal happiness.

My good friend, Mark Harvey, you opened my eyes to a new world of knowledge and possibilities by pressuring me into going to the Millionaire Mind Intensive Conference and convincing me to part way with several thousand pounds to see Tony Robbins; for your relentless selling and badgering, I thank you. You gave me a 'real-life' example (he'll love what I've done there) of someone I know going from financially trapped to financially free.

Additionally, a huge thank you to my mentors, T. Harv Eker, Tony Robbins, Grant Cardone, Russell Brunsen, Paul

O'Mahony, Tai Lopez, Jay Shetty, Alex Mandossian, Gary Vaynerchuck, Clarke Kegley, plus many more who educate me daily.

And, finally, to my beautiful partner, Naomi. You found me in one of my lowest times, where I had all but given up and accepted that I had to settle for a life of mediocrity.

You supported me in believing that there was more to life than working all week and 'living' at the weekend. You bring out the best in me.

This book marks just one of the many accomplishments that we will achieve together.

ABOUT THE AUTHOR

Jason Staniforth is a self-professed marketing and technology addict who truly believes that the more you can help people, the more money you will make.

Coming from a Psychology background, Jason stumbled into a career in marketing, but very quickly embraced the fast-paced and ever-evolving landscape in order to achieve great success.

By the age of 23, Jason had created, and was heading up, the marketing function for a multi-million-pound print solutions company. That organisation has gone on to be the largest independent print solutions company in the UK and has recently been bought by a global print-tech company.

Since then, Jason has devoted much of his working career to mastering the beast that is marketing, exploring every possible avenue to ensure that he remains current and informed. As well as focusing on creating multiple streams of passive income for himself, he has continued to help many organisations, and new business start-ups, to build a foundation in which they can grow from.

In his spare time, Jason goes to the gym, walks his dog, spends time with his partner, Naomi, and visits his family.

TESTIMONIALS

I started speaking with Jay when he reached out to my cry for help on social media. He offered his expert advice to help me with marketing my charity for anxiety sufferers which, at the time, was really struggling and its future wasn't looking great.

Jay shared his story with me about his experience with anxiety and, funnily enough, mentioned this book that he was writing – I instantly knew he was the right guy for the job! I explained how we were struggling to raise awareness of the cause and also to generate funds. Jay instantly added value to our charity! He did this through consultation sessions where he provided me with valuable ideas and tasks to improve our situation. He was so positive, and it really encouraged me to push myself and, overall, I have noticed such a big difference.

Engagement across our social media channels has grown to an impressive level in a very short space of time, and it only shows signs of continuing to grow as I apply the techniques Jay has taught me. In addition to this, his guidance on branding and our website has helped turn what before could only be described as a hard-to-navigate notice board, into an email and donation-generating machine.

Jay's lesson and techniques have given the charity a new lease of life and have contributed greatly to its continuation which, in turn, enables us to help even more people in need.

Michelle – UK Anxiety Charity

Working with Jay has been invaluable to the success of my business. In just a few consultations, Jay helped me to systemise my marketing strategy, funnels, and track the performance of every campaign. Not only that, but he also completely transformed my phone sales process, helping me to achieve a 90% conversion rate and making over £19k within just one week.

Jay has helped me to identify my company vision, and customer avatar, to heighten my company's conversions though more specific marketing and ensuring we are attracting the customers that are right for me.

With being an online fitness business, and the market being so saturated, Jay has helped me to take things to the next level; but even with all this success, the most valuable part, for me, is his customer care, support, and passion for what he does.

Stephen – Online, celebrity fitness coach

AFFIRMATION

This is a power statement that you should say out loud every single day.

To perform this affirmation, or 'declaration' as some people call them, you place your hand on your heart and speak the words:

This is my dream,

my passion,

my purpose,

and now my goal,

and I am fully committed to making this work,

no matter what challenge I face,

no matter how many times I stumble or fall,

this is my destiny,

this is the first step to creating a new me,

a better me,

and a more successful version of me.

www.empire-consulting.co.uk

Printed in Poland
by Amazon Fulfillment
Poland Sp. z o.o., Wrocław